A Letter
To
My Grandchildren

GEORGE M. BROCKWAY, PH.D.

authorHOUSE®

AuthorHouse™
1663 Liberty Drive
Bloomington, IN 47403
www.authorhouse.com
Phone: 1 (800) 839-8640

Published by AuthorHouse 05/01/2019

ISBN: 978-1-7283-0809-8 (sc)
ISBN: 978-1-7283-0808-1 (e)

Library of Congress Control Number: 2019904337

Print information available on the last page.

This book is printed on acid-free paper.

CONTENTS

As I write this letter, my grandchildren's ages are 22, 17, 15 and 12, and my great niece and nephew's ages are 15 and 13.

All, except perhaps the two youngest, are capable of reading the words in this letter but they may not all be capable, at this time in their lives, of fully understanding the letter. But that's all right, it'll be waiting for them when they are ready, maybe tucked away in the back of a drawer somewhere or stuck between two books on a bookshelf.

And, of course, beyond being capable of understanding what's here, there is the issue of being interested in what's here. I am fully aware that it would be foolhardy of me to assume much interest on their part *at this time in their lives.* Though maybe there will be some, just because it's addressed to them? Or perhaps because their grandfather/gruncle (great uncle) wrote it? Or perhaps because most of the various quotes throughout are fun to read? Who knows? But I do harbor some hope that it won't go completely unremarked.

Alert: to the grandchildren and great niece and nephew: I am writing to your adult selves, both that part which is already present in you and that which is yet to come. It may involve a style of reading and thinking which you're not very used to. I hope you'll give it a chance.

INTRODUCTION

Dear Jake and Maddie, Grace and Cal and Ingrid and Ivan,

I've got two reasons for writing you this 'letter': the first is to let you know something about me, your grandpa (or great uncle) before I "shuffle off this mortal coil". But the second and more important is to, hopefully, spark some thoughts in you and maybe even cause you to open a 'door' to possibilities you may not have, heretofore, contemplated.

Those possibilities, really <u>that</u> possibility, is of a spiritual realm. This is a bit hard to define but is not to be confused with the *humanistic spiritual*; the 'spiritual' of: art, music and literature. Those aspects of our human personalities which resonate with and seek out the beautiful, the ecstatic, the uplifting, in any of those activities. All of which are wonderful and worth seeking and experiencing. But I am speaking here of some sort of *religious spiritual*. A realm if you will, a level of reality, which underlies, encompasses and expands upon our everyday physical levels of reality. A level of reality which is <u>not</u> accessible to our senses. (And this last point is HUGE!, but I'll wait until later to say much about it and even then I'll *t r y* to avoid too much philosophical jibber-jabber. But cut me some slack, old codgers do tend to go on and I am, after all, <u>your</u> old codger.)

Often this other realm, this religious spiritual realm, is referred to in a kind of shorthand by calling it God or Allah or Yahweh, Brahman, or Rigpa, the Absolute Space of Phenomena (dharmadhatu), the Fundamental Mind of Clear Light or the Continuum of Consciousness. **But however it is called, it refers to a wider, deeper, all pervasive *reality* within which we live and move and have our being <u>and</u> which determines the final meaning and value of what we do and of what we become.**

That's a mouthful. But focus on the last sentence in the preceding paragraph. That's huge and <u>that's</u> what we're going to be talking about. That's big, really, r e a l l y BIG. If it's true, it's hard to imagine anything more important. And if it's not true, it would be really important to know that as well. But why would it be important? Why should you care?

1

In a 'word', because the truth matters. It's obvious that it does so in most or all of our normal, daily living. From the truth about how much gas you have left in the car's gas tank to whether that food you want to eat is contaminated to whether you can trust your friend to keep a confidence. It matters.

Similarly, it matters in this area, in the area of what's real and whether that includes a spiritual realm, a spiritual reality. Though here, it may be harder to see that it matters, that it makes a difference, and harder to see what that difference is. An allegory may help you understand the kind of difference it could make.

Imagine that you were born blind or by some accident became blind very shortly after your birth. Now, 25 years later, there's been a medical breakthrough and it is possible for you to gain or regain your sight. Wow! What would you now see and how would you react? Suddenly, you could for the first time see colors and shapes, you could actually see and experience what "near" and "far" meant, and how objects were spatially related. From a no-color world to one of technicolor, from a flat world to one of infinite dimensions, new connections between felt shapes and seen shapes. Your experience would be sooooo much richer, more full-bodied, more full of connections and implications than you could even have imagined before gaining sight. Indeed, it would be so new and unexpected that initially it would be disconcerting and unsettling. So unsettling, in fact, that you might prefer to go back to the way you were. (There are actual instances of just this: people who suddenly gain/regain their sight and are so discombobulated by the experience that they express the desire to go back to the way things were before, when they were blind.) But no, here you are with a whole new and richer way of seeing the world if you'll just open to it.

(N.B. the most famous allegory meant to illustrate a similar point is in Plato's *Republic*, his allegory of the cave: 514a-517a. You absolutely <u>can't</u> go wrong by reading it since you will see it referenced and alluded to throughout the rest of your lives. Might just as well see what all the fuss is about.)

Similarly, the difference that coming to 'see' or accept that there really is a spiritual realm can be huge, both life altering and life enriching. But is this the sort of thing, you (or anyone) <u>can</u> *know*? Or is it something nobody knows, and so you can just pick any side you want or even ignore it all together?

I think it is something you can (come to) *know* and, in large part, that's what this letter is going to be about. About how people have come to *know* in this area, about how <u>you</u> might come to *know* about this.

So here's the way I'm going to structure this letter. I'm going to look at some of the most common ways people have taken in the past to make their own decisions regarding such a spiritual realm. Let's call it the *religious spiritual realm, (RSR for short),* to distinguish it from that *humanistic spiritual* that I referred to earlier. But this review of some of the classical ways of trying to answer this question is <u>not</u> going to be a scholarly thesis, so you can relax, r e l a x x x. Rather, it'll be more a matter of my mentioning or pointing them out and saying just a little about them. If you get interested in any of them there are plenty of resources you can go to to learn more. And I'll mention some of those resources as we go along.

Here are the five ways of approaching this subject that I'm going to review. I'm putting them here because I'll use them as headings throughout the letter and you can then just skip to whichever one you're most interested in at that point in time. **Family up-bringing; Apologetics; An Experience of; The Views (conclusions?) of Significant Others** (this one will be done throughout rather than as a separate section); and **Individual Questions.** (And if this 'letter' gets to be long enough, I'll probably make a table of contents and put page numbers to make it even easier to skip to where you want to be.)

Of these five different approaches, I'm most intrigued and excited by the last one: Individual Questions. We'll see if I can pull it off. When you get there, you tell me.

<u>WHAT OTHER PEOPLE THINK</u>

But first, a disclaimer. The fact that some person, let's call him Albert, thinks that something is so, is not, usually, a good argument for thinking that it <u>is</u> so. (The exception would be when Albert is an expert in a particular field, e.g. physics, and what he is talking about deals with something in that field. And even then, the mere fact that Albert thinks that it is so, is not, by itself, any proof that it actually is so.) Thus, I do not include the quotes that appear throughout this letter as any kind of proof that there is more to what exists than simply the material or that something transcendent* actually does exist. Rather, they are simply meant to show that some intelligent, reflective and knowledgeable people think these things are so. And if some intelligent, reflective and knowledgeable people think that they are so, you certainly would not be silly or dumb, deluded or naive to at least wonder about whether they <u>are</u> true or not . . . . or even, imagine that, looking into it.

> (And if you don't know who the person being quoted is, I strongly recommend you look them up. I think you'll often be surprised, and impressed.)

And one last comment on the structure of the 'letter'. It is NOT meant to be read straight through, the way you might read a novel. In fact, I'm going to put a little line of symbols ✳✳✳✳✳✳✳ at the bottom of any section or page where I think you should STOP READING, (actually put the letter down, maybe even close your eyes, and just *think*, think about what I've just said. Just, . . . *think* about it. Ask yourself: what does *that* mean? Or, *how* does that affect me? In fact, *does* it affect me? Suppose it <u>is</u> true, what then? A really, really different way of reading, hmm? And you don't have to wait for that line of symbols to do it. But that's ok, it's a letter and there won't be any test on it. So let's get started.

* Hmmmmm. I suspect, before we really get into it, I need to say a bit more about what I mean by the *transcendent* since I will sometimes use that term to refer to the *religious spiritual* realm.

4

What I'm referring to by *transcendent* is something that exists, e.g. it can and does have an effect outside of itself, but it exists above and beyond the physical, material reality we interact with all the time in our daily lives. It is "beyond" the physical in that it is not physical at all, there is no materiality to it. It can't be touched or known through any of our five senses. It can't be cut or divided or broken down physically in any way. It is simply not physical or material. (I'm using those two terms: 'physical' and 'material' as synonyms for now.)

And it is "above" the physical in that it is not limited or constrained by those things that characterize or define anything physical/material. Thus it has no physical dimensions or weight or color, it is not rough or smooth, slippery or sticky, etc.. It is not limited by location or size or weight or time or distance. It is really quite other than any of the physical/material reality we constantly interact with.

Okaayyyyy, you might be saying to yourself about now, but does anything like that actually exist? And how would/could we ever know it if it did? BINGO! That's exactly what I want to talk with you about. I'm sooo glad you asked those questions. ;-)

"It is FLAT-OUT strange that something–that *anything*– is happening at all.

There was nothing, then a Big Bang, then here we all are. This is extremely weird. To Schelling's burning question, "Why is there something rather than nothing?," there have always been two general answers. The first might be called the philosophy of "oops." The universe just occurs, there is nothing behind it, it's all ultimately accidental or random, it just is, it just happens– oops! The philosophy of oops, no matter how sophisticated and adult it may on occasion appear– its modern names and numbers are legion, from positivism to scientific materialism, from linguistic analysis to historical materialism, from naturalism to empiricism– always comes down to the same basic answer, namely, "Don't ask." The question itself (Why is anything at all happening? Why am I here?)– the *question itself* is said to be confused, pathological, nonsensical, or infantile. To stop asking such silly or confused questions is, they all maintain, the mark of maturity, the sign of growing up in this cosmos. . . . . . .

. . . The other broad answer that has been tendered is that *something else* is going on: behind the happenstance drama is a deeper or higher or wider pattern, or order, or intelligence. There are, of course, many varieties of this "Deeper Order": the Tao, God, Geist, Maat, Archetypal Forms, Reason, Li, Mahamaya, Brahman, Rigpa. And although these different varieties of the Deeper Order certainly disagree with each other at many points, they all agree on this: the universe is not what it appears. *Something else is going on*, something quite other than oops. . . ."

– Ken Wilber[1]

FAMILY UP-BRINGING

As it happens, the swamping majority of people in the world come to their view(s) on this issue of whether or not there actually is any *religious spiritual reality* or *RSR*, by being raised to think one way or the other. Usually their parents, reinforced by their culture or the schools they go to or their extended family, have a certain viewpoint on this issue and convey that viewpoint to their children. Sometimes that conveying is done explicitly and with more or less conviction, sometimes it's done simply by osmosis. We believe a particular way because those whom we think of as knowledgeable and intelligent tell us or imply that this is the way things are. And when we are young, we have no other equally respected source to go to.

But often, and maybe it's already happened to you, as we get older, especially when we leave the family nest and head out into the wider world, whether to college or simply start living independently on our own, we begin to question those beliefs that we took for granted because they came from our parents. Or it might happen in high school when we encounter other kids who believe differently, or teachers who do so. (And it may even happen because you've got a pushy grandfather who prods you to think about weird stuff!)

And in most of these family contexts, when the conviction is that <u>there is</u> a *religious spiritual*, the ultimate support for such views is usually some supposedly revealed or sacred text, whether the Bible, the Qur'an, the Rig Veda and Upanishads of Hinduism, the Pali Canon of Buddhism, the Hebrew Bible of Judaism, the Tao Te Ching, etc.. And in some of those cases (the Western monotheisms, e.g.), the text is not just revered and honored, it is thought to have been transmitted or revealed in some way by God, or Allah or Yahweh.

And believers therefore think that what it says must be true. (Though there can be and usually is a lot of controversy over how its words are to be taken or understood. Are they meant literally as in an instruction manual or metaphorically as in a story? And since such texts were usually written thousands of years ago, there are questions about what the words used in writing them meant to their authors and the people reading them back then.)

So, family up-bringing and "revealed" texts are undoubtedly the most common ways in which people <u>world wide</u> come to believe the way they do about a *spiritual* realm. And that was certainly the case with me. I was raised to believe in God and in a *religious spiritual* realm. My parents were Catholic (my father converted to Catholicism in order to marry my mother) and during my childhood years to age 18, our family were practicing Catholics. We went to church every week. In addition, I went to Catholic schools from first grade through sophomore year in high school. So I had been pretty fully indoctrinated so to speak. I didn't really question the basic tenets of Catholicism during those years. (That changed considerably later on and I would not consider myself to be a Catholic in any traditional sense, today.)

But the opposite could just as easily have been true. I may have been raised to think that there was nothing spiritual, no spiritual realm at all. Not many, in my era, were raised that way. I think it is a much more common way of being raised today. The ethos of America and of Western Europe today is much more one of science and of what science knows as defining both what is and what can be known, than it was 78 years ago. You are growing up in a quite different culture in that regard than what I grew up in.

And although science has brought us many wonderful things and has improved our standard of living remarkably, I fear that a too lock-step adherence to its methods <u>and assumptions</u> may keep people from exploring the full range of what is and of what can be known.

"Science studies the natural. That is all we ask of it. If there is any fact or truth beyond nature, science knows nothing about it and has nothing to say on the subject."

– Richard W. Metz[2]

So, and in the service of full disclosure, I should let you know where I'm coming from as I write you this letter. For a long, long time now (from perhaps as early as my 20th year) I have been convinced of three things. (Some might say "driven by" these three things.) The first is that there is a truth. The world, reality, anything and everything that exists, exists in some way. And the truth is whatever accurately captures and expresses what that way is. This does not preclude change, it's not saying that anything that is, is the way it is forever and ever. Rather, it's saying something more like: at any given point in time, a 'thing', a state of affairs, is what it is and is not something else.

The second thing that has governed much of my activity, much of my life, is the conviction that we can come to know what that truth is. But this second conviction has many qualifications attached to it. I may not be able to know what any particular truth is. Even for those I'm interested in, I may simply not have the smarts. And there may be ways of knowing which I am not privy to or have not developed the skills necessary to employ. And, of course, there may be truths which are simply beyond our (human's) capacities to know. But generally, and as a first approach, I think that we can come to know what is so.

And the third conviction that pervades my thinking is that living in accord with what is true, living in accord with the way 'things' really are, is the best way to live. It is the way of living that will result in the best overall outcome, for me, for society, for the world. But, as with the second conviction spoken of above, there are qualifications that must be admitted. Having this conviction does not mean that I always act this way. I am certainly subject to all the same foibles and frailties that most humans share. (Buddhists refer to these foibles and frailties as "hindrances and obscurations.") Just ask anyone who knows me. (No, no, on second thought, don't do that.) It's largely a matter of believing, of being convinced that, living in accord with what's true must make some *positive* difference.

All of which brings us back to you. The family up-bringing stage of your lives is about over or fairly soon will be. In a "This I Believe" kind of moment, where would you say you are, right now, with respect to your own beliefs about any *religious spiritual realm*, about any sort of transcendent realm or reality? And do you think it would make any difference one way or the other in your life if such existed? Do you think it's something you can ever come to know?

The Take Away: Hmmm. Here's something to think about. Something pretty big and serious. You don't have to dedicate your life to the inquiry, certainly not now. But it might be worth thinking about once and awhile. There may be something to it, and maybe it would make a big difference if it turns out to be true. Indeed, what <u>do</u> you believe about this right now?

"All that I have learned has led me step by step to an unshakable conviction of the existence of God. I only believe in what I know. And that eliminates believing. Therefore I do not take his existence on belief – I know that he exists."

– Carl Jung[3]

"This [Jung's position as stated above] was not a "blind faith", as Dawkins has argued, but (according to Jung) a certainty that is based on evidence. His practice as a psychotherapist and his mythological research had convinced him of God's existence."

– Steve Myers[4]

In what follows, I'll walk with you through some of the views, thoughts and considerations I've encountered in my own search for what's true in this area. In addition to telling you something about me, I'm hoping that it might also be of some help to you in your own searching.

APOLOGETICS

Woahhh, that's a bit ominous sounding. And a word that's probably unfamiliar to you. It simply means trying to establish (or defend) the existence of God by way of reasoning and argumentation. But say to yourself: "be still my heart," because I'm not going to actually be doing much of that here. I'll mention some examples and recount some stories that illustrate it, but it's not going to be a major focus.

My reason for approaching apologetics in this way is twofold: it's a huge topic and there are books and books and books dealing with it. And many of them deal with it better than I ever could. If what I say here sparks your interest, there are many places for you to go to learn more about it, and I will mention a few in the process. The second reason for not getting into this approach in any comprehensive or deep fashion is that doing so would, I think, r e a l l y turn you off. As it does for many people. The arguments, pro and con, are usually abstract, technical, arcane and, frankly, difficult. To the person of casual interest or just getting into the topic, they can be a real interest killer.

Story:

So let me start by simply recounting some stories of people who did approach the issue in that way. And the first such will be about yours truly. I mentioned, above, that I was raised in a believing tradition up through high school. Then I went to college for a year at Holy Cross College in Worcester, MA.. (They had all men's colleges back then, and Holy Cross was one of them.) After a year of college, I entered the Jesuit religious order to start training to become a Jesuit priest.

Flash ahead a couple of years in that training program (through the novitiate) to the second big decision point (the first big one being the decision to enter at all). And that second big point was the decision to take vows or not. Taking vows would continue the training program and officially establish me as a member of the Jesuit religious order. Vows, in this context, refer to solemn promises to God and before your peers and teachers. These vows are vows of poverty (in the Jesuits, this was interpreted to mean that you couldn't own anything though you would be given (to use but not to own) whatever you needed to do your work), chastity (to give up any and all sexual activity forever), and obedience (to obey your superiors as the pragmatic conduit for God's will for you in whatever the circumstance was). It was a big deal. It's those vows that make anyone an official member of any religious order within the Catholic tradition.

Anyway, as I approached the time for those vows (I was 21), it dawned on me that I had never really questioned whether or not God existed. Pretty astounding. Here I was, about to make these solemn promises to God and I had never really questioned whether such a God even existed or not! Woah! That was pretty disconcerting and unsettling. What could/ should I do? It was only a couple of months until I was to take the vows.

Well, the first thing I did was consult one of our more respected teachers to see if he had ever gone through the same sort of doubt and questioning. And to my surprise, he had <u>not.</u> 'What??!' I thought, 'how could you not have questioned whether or not God existed?' And this guy was no slouch in the intellectual arena. A Ph.D. in the classics from Harvard University as well as all the other degrees one got by going through the Jesuit training back then. But I set aside my surprise and dismay and decided I'd just have to investigate the question on my own. We had a good library. I could read and think, I'd just get to it.

And one of the authors I read during this period was John Henry (Cardinal) Newman (1801-1890). An Anglican priest who converted to

Catholicism and was later made a Cardinal in the Catholic Church. Also a very bright guy who had a wonderful writing style to boot. And so, I read a couple of his better known works: *Grammar of Assent and Apologia Pro Vita Sua*, looking for some help in answering the question that was so troubling me. And I found it there (I forget now, in which of those books I found it). But his approach to my question satisfied me at the time and relieved my doubts and concerns about taking my vows.

I'm telling you this story because Newman's approach was an example of apologetics, albeit a fairly simple and easily understood example of it. Basically, and as I remember it, his argument went like this:

Something exists now, so something must always have existed.

(Because you can't get something from nothing.)

And we have a choice, we can decide that that something which has always existed is matter (today, we'd probably say: the matter-energy dyad), or it's intelligence.

'To me,' Cardinal Newman said, 'intelligence seems the much more likely candidate.'

And I agreed with him. It seemed the much more likely candidate to me also. And it still does. (And apparently, not just to me. See the next page.)

So I went ahead and took my vows.

"Another source of conviction in the existence of God, connected with the reason and not with the feelings, impresses me as having much more weight. This follows from the extreme difficulty or rather impossibility of conceiving this immense and wonderful universe, including man with his capacity of looking far backward and far into futurity, as the result of blind chance or necessity. When thus reflecting I feel compelled to look to a First Cause having an intelligent mind in some degree analogous to that of man; and I deserve to be called a Theist."

– Charles Darwin[5]

"It is enough for me to contemplate the mystery of conscious life perpetuating itself through all eternity, to reflect upon the marvelous structure of the universe which we dimly perceive, and to try humbly to comprehend an infinitesimal part *of the intelligence manifested in nature.*" [emph. mine]

– Albert Einstein[6]

"God is what mind becomes when it has passed beyond the scale of our comprehension."

– Freeman Dyson[7]

The first gulp from the glass of natural sciences will make you an atheist, but at the bottom of the glass God is waiting for you.

– Werner Heisenberg
(As often attributed.)

But there are also many smart men and women who would and do disagree with Newman's argument. That's one of the features of apologetics. The arguments are pro and con and, usually, for every pro argument there is a con argument. As a result, it can be a confusing and even discouraging approach to the question. Though it can also be enlightening and definitely not one to be discarded lightly.

So, I'll give you some ideas, some directions you might want to go in, and then we'll move on to people's **experiences of or with the religious spiritual or the transcendent.** But actually, before I do that, here's another story you might enjoy.

Story:

Another approach via apologetics is illustrated in Francis Collins's book: *The Language of God.* Collins is the director of the National Institutes of Health and was /is the head of the Human Genome Project. (Not bad for science credentials, hmm?) He recounts, in his book, how he moved from agnosticism to atheism early in his life to being a believer later on. It's a fun story to follow. In his case, he found the pivotal difference maker in a book by C. S. Lewis, (yes, that same C. S. Lewis who wrote *The Chronicles of Narnia and The Space Trilogy*). The book was Lewis's *Mere Christianity.* And the argument that stopped Collins in his tracks and caused him to rethink (and eventually change) his position was an argument from the presence of what Lewis called **the moral law** in each of us. I.e. the fact that virtually everyone thinks that there is a moral right or wrong, ways of acting that are morally right or morally wrong, and feels obligated to act according to the morally good and guilty if he/she has acted in a morally wrong way. To Lewis, and Collins after him, the experience of this universal moral law or imperative was best explained as a sign or an indication that a loving and a just God existed. This just <u>was</u> God revealing him/herself to us.

Ah haaa! You might think. All of that can now be explained by socio-biology and cultural conditioning. But Lewis and Collins were aware of those arguments and present counter-arguments to refute them. But I am

NOT going to go into all those arguments here. My only point was to recount Collins's story as another example of someone who was moved to change his belief system by a kind of apologetics.

So, if argument and counter-argument are your instinctual or preferred ways of approaching a subject, you might look into apologetics. Probably the classic example of apologetics occurs early in St. Thomas Aquinas's *Summa Theologiae* and is commonly referred to as "the five ways". There are many, many books on these five ways which you can find simply by googling the topic. But for a very short and interesting summary and commentary on the five ways you might look at Karen Armstrong's *The Case for God*, pp. 142-146. And here are a couple more books that deal with God (or the spiritual realm) in an apologetics kind of way: *How To Think About God* by Mortimer Adler. A relatively easy read, a good overview, and some worthwhile insights. Another would be Alvin Plantinga's *God and Other Minds*. A much, much more difficult read, but incredibly well argued. Both are on the pro side, but they both cite and respond to other authors who are on the con side.

The take away: arguments can be put forward, both pro and con, for the existence of God or a *religious spiritual realm,* but no one of them has ever convinced everyone. On the other hand, and assuming argument is your preferred way of approaching things, you don't need to find an argument that will convince everyone, you only need to find one that convinces you one way or the other. Well, . . . one that convinces you *and* that holds up to at least some moderate scrutiny.

AN EXPERIENCE

(As a way of opening that 'door'.)

Of Consciousness Itself

OK, so what's puzzling about consciousness? How could it be evidence for something that exists but is not material nor dependent upon the material for its existence (e.g. a *religious spiritual realm*)?

I think the easiest way of 'seeing' what's puzzling about consciousness is to reflect on some of the ways in which it seems so different from anything material. As examples of conscious events, just think of your own thoughts about what you will do tomorrow for example, or a memory of what you did last week, or your thoughts about why it's good to be kind to people. None of these thoughts has any physical characteristics, no size or shape or color, they don't exert any gravitational force. They can't be seen under even the most powerful microscope. There is nothing physical about them. So how could something physical, the brain e.g., create them? How could something which has all those physical characteristics create/cause something which has none of them? Another way of asking this question is: how can something give what it doesn't have?

> "We [Buddhists] say that consciousness is produced from consciousness. Consciousness must be produced from consciousness because it cannot be produced with matter as its substantial cause. Particles cannot create an entity of luminosity and knowing. Matter cannot be the substantial cause of consciousness . . . . There is no way to posit consciousness except as being a continuation of former moments of consciousness; in this way consciousness can have no beginning . . ."
>
> – Dalai Lama[8]

"According to *standard materialistic doctrine*, consciousness, like space-time before the invention of general relativity, plays a secondary, subservient role, being considered just a function of matter and a tool for the description of the truly existing material world. But let us remember that our knowledge of the world begins **not** with matter but with perceptions. I know for sure that my pain exists, my "green" exists, and my "sweet" exists. I do not need any proof of their existence, because these events are a part of me; everything else is a theory." [emph. mine]

– Andrei Linde[9]

Well now, that's pretty strange isn't it? Because most people certainly *think* that their brain is what's causing their thoughts, memories, plans, hopes, fears, etc.. And here, such a view is not just being questioned, it's being denied. How could it be that consciousness is <u>not</u> caused by the brain?

Here's just one possibility. Think of the brain as like a radio receiver which responds to radio waves and enables us to hear what those waves are conveying. It doesn't create the radio waves, but it's necessary if we are to hear them and react to them. Maybe the brain is like that. Maybe we need a brain to receive and to interpret consciousness in our present, embodied state, but it doesn't create consciousness any more than the radio receiver creates the radio waves.

I'm not saying it <u>is</u> this way, only that it could be and that would explain how it's possible to have conscious experience which is, nevertheless, <u>not</u> caused by the brain. So consciousness itself, something with which we are more intimately acquainted than with anything else in our lives, <u>is</u> curious.

> "Is it possible that . . . consciousness may exist by itself, even in the absence of matter, just like gravitational waves, excitations of space, may exist in the absence of protons and electrons?"
>
> – Andrei Linde[10]

The take away: we already have **an experience of** something that exists – a something which is, in fact, closer to us and more obvious to us, than anything else in the world – namely, our own consciousness – and that something is not material (at least as we experience it, it is not) and nor need it be dependent upon the material for its existence. Woahhh, . . . think about *that*.

Aside from our experience of consciousness itself, there are **other experiences** that people have (claimed to have) had, which are *quite out of the ordinary* and are often taken as evidence for something *transcendent*, something *spiritual* in the religious sense of the term. And these experiences are wide spread enough that we should pay at least some attention to them.

Basically, someone claims that they have experienced something transcendent or some transcendent reality. Some reality which involves the existence of a non-physical realm. Something that can't be explained by the ordinary laws of science as we understand them today. Stated in that fashion, it's a pretty broad category. It would encompass everything from ghosts and spirits to shamanic spirit animals, miracles, appearances, near death experiences, out of body experiences, the siddhis of Buddhism and Hinduism, mystical states of consciousness and the similar (same?) states of consciousness brought about by entheogens (psychedelic drugs).

That's a lot. And I suspect that if we were to try to consider each one individually you would, fairly quickly, get caught up in and get lost in the details. So I'll focus on just a few of these unusual kinds of experiences.

But before I do, I want to look at the general framework within which we tend to approach <u>all</u> of these different kinds of experiences. People claim that they have had a particular experience. An experience that is of, or requires, some kind of non-physical reality. Sometimes these experiences, or the person having them, are being simultaneously observed by others who are not having the experience in question. And in some of these cases, the person having the experience has a very difficult time articulating exactly what it was that they experienced. But even in those cases, there is virtual unanimity among them that they experienced something *transcendent*, something real that cannot be explained simply by empirical methods.

The non-experiencer in these cases (you and me, for example) is left with two big questions:

1) has the person who had the experience <u>described</u> <u>what they experienced</u> <u>accurately</u>? And,

2) is what the person claims to have experienced real, i.e. does it exist independently of the mind of the experiencer? Is it something *perceived* by the mind vs. something *created* by the mind?

In that sense, is it revelatory or is it illusory? It would be illusory if the experiencer thinks it's real– i.e. exists independently of her own mind– but it doesn't. And it would be revelatory if it presented something to the experiencer that existed independently of them. Very important questions, but can they be answered? How?

But isn't this situation comparable to the situation where you feel that a significant other in your life (your mother or father e.g., or a spouse or lover) really loves you? Have you described your experience (the feeling-experience of being loved) accurately? And is that experience wholly generated by you or is it truly an experience *of* something which is, at least in part, independent of you? You, most commonly, have no doubt that it is an experience <u>of</u> something that is not generated wholly within your own mind. But could you ever convince a skeptical other of that?

So let's go on.

OK, enough of the philosophical questions and puzzles for now. Let's get back to the sorts of **experiences** that are typically involved here. I'll focus on three such: so-called miracles, out of body experiences, and mystical states of consciousness.

<u>MIRACLES</u>

"It is therefore inaccurate to define a miracle as something that breaks the laws of Nature. It doesn't. . . . The divine art of miracle is not an art of suspending the pattern to which events conform but of feeding new events into that pattern. It does not violate the law's proviso, 'If A, then B': it says, 'But this time instead of A, A2,' and Nature, speaking through all her laws, replies 'Then B2'and naturalizes the immigrant, as she well knows how. . . . A miracle is emphatically not an event without cause or without results. Its cause is the activity of God; its results follow according to Natural law."

– C. S. Lewis[11]

There are many different kinds of miracles and different historical time-frames in which they are alleged to have occurred. So we have the various miracles talked about in the Bible and we have miracles that are claimed to have occurred since biblical times. There are miracles that involve the changing of physical substances (water into wine, multiplication of the loaves and fishes etc.), miracles that contravene or transcend physical laws (raising the dead, defying gravity, etc.) and miracles that involve healing or appearances among others.

Yeah, but did these alleged miracles really occur? And is there really no way they could have happened naturally? Legitimate questions and ones which should be asked in each and every case of an alleged miracle. The Catholic Church, for example, takes these exact questions really, really seriously and subjects any claim of a miracle to a very long and extensive analysis and investigation. And only those (very few) which pass such rigorous investigations are finally accepted as miracles. It seems to come down to: 'well, neither we (nor anyone else) can come up with a *more plausible* explanation of how this might have occurred naturally, so we'll accept that it occurred supernaturally' i.e. as a result of some supernatural input. (Please note that I'm <u>not</u> saying that because the Catholic Church says it's a genuine miracle, it is so. I'm only pointing out that even the Church which would stand to gain from such a claim being accepted, recognizes the necessity of vetting any such claim very, very carefully.)

For now, I'll just talk about two different kinds of miracles: **appearances and healings**. Both easy to understand and relatively plentiful in their alleged occurrence. Examples of **<u>appearances</u>** would be those at Lourdes or Fatima or Guadalupe (in the Catholic tradition).

So let's take as our example what is alleged to have occurred in Guadalupe (Mexico) back in 1531. A Mexican peasant named Juan Diego had a vision of a young woman at a place called the Hill of Tepeyac. This woman identified herself to Juan as the Virgin Mary, "the mother of the true deity." And she spoke to Juan in his native tongue, not Spanish. His native tongue was Nahuatl, the language of the Aztec empire. This woman referred to herself as being revered in the Spaniards' religion, apparently something he was not a part of as he was not a Catholic. And she asked that a church be built on that site in her religion's honor.

Juan then went to report the appearance to the archbishop of Mexico City at that time, a Fray Juan de Zumárraga, who, not surprisingly, thinks the whole thing is bunk and asks Juan to request of this lady in the appearance that she provide some unmistakable sign to prove her identity. Juan goes back to the place of the apparition, sees the lady again and relays the archbishop's request, which she says she will grant.

There is other stuff going on in Juan's life that complicates the story and involves some healing of and appearances to his uncle, but skipping to the gist of the story, the lady tells Juan to go to the top of Tepeyac hill which was normally barren, especially in December, and pick the flowers he would find there. Juan went to the top of the hill and finds Castilian roses blooming there, a flower not native to Mexico. The Virgin arranges the flowers in Juan's cloak and when he goes back to the archbishop to reveal the sign she has given and opens his cloak, the flowers fall out and there is an image of the Virgin on the fabric of his cloak. This cloak with the image is now preserved in The Basilica of Our Lady of Guadalupe in Mexico City, and both it, and the story behind it, have played a large and significant role in Mexican Catholicism and, indeed, in Mexican history.

At the time and subsequently there was much doubt and skepticism among the church leaders about what really occurred and whether the story or the cloak's image could be trusted. But it has certainly come to be honored and revered among Mexican Catholics, and Juan Diego was, eventually (2002!), canonized (judged by the Church to have reported accurately what he encountered and to have subsequently interceded in other miracles, usually healings).

In any case, this alleged occurrence typifies the way most appearances unfold. In such cases, some person (or persons) claim to have encountered someone who no longer exists in any physical or bodily way. In the cases just mentioned, these interactions take place a number of times and involve communication between the observer(s) and the apparition. Jesus's appearances to his followers after his crucifixion and death would probably also be put into this category.

And then there are mysterious **healings**. Cases where people have diagnosed and confirmed illnesses that are often either life-threatening or severely debilitating. Then they have a vision or undergo a laying-on of hands or simply are the object of someone(s) prayers and, mysteriously, get better. The doctors who were attending them can't explain it. There was a tumor or a cancer, it wasn't responding to conventional treatments and now, somehow, it's gone. And there is a specific sequence to the happenings: they were prayed for and subsequently got better; or there was a laying-on of hands and they subsequently got better. It looks like the first *caused* the second; certainly it's the standard sequence in which cause and effect work. But there are often, in these cases, possible or even plausible alternative explanations for the cure, yet there are enough where the medical experts *can't* explain how it happened to at least open one to the possibility of some non-physical agency at work. Something entirely non-detectable by empirical measures and instruments which nevertheless can have an effect in the physical world. An occurrence, incidentally, which is absolutely ruled out by materialists, not, however, by argument but by presumption. (A "materialist" is someone who believes that the only thing that exists is matter or what is equivalent to matter (energy), and everything that we can and do experience is in someway wholly dependent upon a material cause. Thus a materialist would deny anything like a *religious spiritual realm/reality*.)

Nor are such miracles confined to the monotheisms of Western culture, though those are the ones I have focused on. In the Eastern religions of Hinduism and Buddhism e.g., there are some things called *siddhis*. These encompass a range of activities, from paranormal abilities like hearing or seeing things that are far away or entering the minds of others, to activities that are definitely beyond the natural, like moving the body wherever thought goes (teleportation, astral projection) or assuming any form desired. But I know so little about these and am so suspicious and skeptical about them that I will not try to deal with them here. In addition, I do not think they count as "miracles" in the usual sense of that term, since they are not alleged to involve any input from a God.

In any case, however, we can at least say, with J.B.S. Haldane (below), that the realm of what exists is apparently much broader than simply the physical, material, universe.

"The Universe is not only queerer than we suppose, but queerer than we can suppose."

– J. B. S. Haldane[12]

OUT OF BODY EXPERIENCES

In addition to the miracles mentioned above, there are what are called out of body experiences (OBE's). A classic example of this would be when someone is on the operating table, completely immobilized and anesthetized, and yet when they are brought back to consciousness after the operation, they report seeing (typically from a ceiling perspective) or hearing some of what went on in the operating theater, or even in some room down the hall! And what they claimed to have seen and heard is corroborated by others who were in the places in question at the time of the sightings and hearings. A variant of this kind of occurrence is when the person on the table has, technically, died, i.e. their heart has stopped and their brain is flat lining. But then they are revived and recount hearing and seeing things that went on during their death period. Very strange stuff, but enough corroborated instances of it to, at least, make one question and wonder.

In all of these latter cases, I think **the main "take-away"** is something more specific than the take-away from appearances or healings. Here I think it is that mind or consciousness is apparently not confined to our bodily space, e.g. to our brains. Think about that. Assume the experiences these people have had are being accurately described. Certainly they are corroborated as such. Is there any way of explaining them *other than* that their consciousness somehow operated outside of and independent of their body?

So, ... **experiences** of various sorts have been a way in which some people have come to believe (and some would say 'know') that there is something that exists which is neither material nor dependent upon the material for its existence. In other words, that there is a *religious spiritual realm or reality.*

❊❊❊❊❊❊❊

And there is one more kind of experience that I want to talk about.

STATES OF MYSTICAL CONSCIOUSNESS

"For me, as both a scientist and a humanist, the transcendent experience is the most powerful evidence we have for a spiritual world. By this I mean the immediate and vital personal experience of being connected to something larger than ourselves, to feeling some unseen order or truth in the world. The experience I had looking up at the stars off the coast of Maine was a transcendent experience. I've had others."

– Alan Lightman[13]

"I remember the night, and almost the very spot on the hilltop, where my soul opened out, as it were, into the Infinite, and there was a rushing together of two worlds, the inner and the outer. It was deep calling unto deep– the deep that my own struggle had opened up within being answered by the unfathomable deep without, reaching beyond the stars. I stood alone with Him who had made me, and all the beauty of the world, and love, and sorrow and even temptation.I did not seek Him, but felt the perfect union of my spirit with His . . . Since that time no discussion that I have heard of the proofs of God's existence has been able to shake my faith. Having once felt the presence of God's spirit, I have never lost it again for long. My most assuring evidence of his existence is deeply rooted in that hour of vision in the memory of that supreme experience."

A clergyman's experience as recounted in
William James's *Varieties of Religious Experience*

This last kind of experience I want to look at is what is usually called a state of mystical consciousness. The quotes by Alan Lightman and the clergyman (above) fall into this category of experience. It's hard to give any generic description of these states of consciousness, partly because they encompass quite a range of experience and partly because what the person claims to have experienced is often quite hard to comprehend. They speak of things far outside our normal, every day experience. But I'll give it a try. And in doing so, I'll focus on mystical states of consciousness as recounted by religious adepts and those in altered states of consciousness caused by the use of psychedelics, now and in this context often referred to as entheogens. (A custom I'll follow here.)

Typically, what seems to happen in these cases of mystical consciousness is an individual, whether in deep meditation or in an ecstatic moment or under the influence of an entheogen, has a particular kind of experience. They come to 'see' (not with their physical eyes obviously) or become aware of a particular way in which 'things' are; i.e. a certain way in which the world (everything that is) exists. In particular, they often also 'see' themselves in a whole new way, as being one with the universe. They have a great sense of wholeness and unification with everything that exists.

One way of describing this state and this realization (though an admittedly dense and arcane "way") has been by saying that: there just is non-dual awareness, and *we* just are, ultimately, non-dual awareness. Another way of saying or describing it has been to say that all subject-object duality is ultimately an illusion.

Tat Tvam Asi
(Sanscrit for '**That thou art**')

From the Hindu Holy Books or Scriptures, the Upanishads, 800-500 B.C.E.!
Hmmm. Maybe some ancient cultures <u>do</u> have something to tell us?

And here is **a story**, <u>and</u> <u>a description</u> from a very good friend of mine who has had just this kind of experience a number of times while in guided trips under the influence of an entheogen.

"My friend.....it is not easy to understand unity without *experiencing* the absence of duality. But let me try this: imagine a great Wall. On one side of the Wall is the land of 'Unity', and the other side of the Wall is the land of 'Duality'. The Wall has a name......it is called 'Self'. The more 'Self' an individual has, the higher the Wall.

The land of Duality is made up of subjects and objects. Human beings live in the land of Duality, and this is quite understandable when one considers millions of years of evolution. It took evolution many years to build a human brain that is designed for propagation and survival. Seeing things dualistically helps keep us from the tigers.

But, of course, if there really is a land of Unity, there can't be a land of Duality, or a Wall of "Self" separating the two, because the land of Unity encompasses Everything. The wall of Self, and the land of Duality, are, at the end of the day, an illusion. And by "illusion" I mean that subject-object duality is not a lasting reality. It is dependent upon having a Self (as subject) and other than Self (as object). One can experience the truth of this illusion when the Self disappears. In my metaphor, the Wall disappears, and the land of Duality is subsumed into the land of Unity. This happens in finer and finer increments, as Self thinks about thinking. At first, it is the thought. Then the thought of the thought, then the thought of the thought of the thought, etc. In metaphorical terms, I saw my Self hanging onto an infinite wall of hard and smooth white ivory. The wall was absolutely perfectly smooth.....not a blemish....except for one small crack that I was desperately holding onto with my fingernails. My first thought was to hold on, or "I" would perish. My next thought was to remember the thought of holding on, and my next thought after that was to remember to remember the thought of holding on, etc. With each iteration of thoughts, the crack was cut in half. With the first thought to hold on, the crack was 'x' wide. With the thought of the thought of holding on, the crack shrank to ½ x. With the thought of the thought of the thought of holding on, the crack shrank to ¼ x and so forth until the crack was infinitely thin. As the process was progressing, my Self was desperately trying to hold on. It was sending me a loud alert that said essentially: "This is NOT good. This is NOT good. I'm dyyiiinnnngggg." But at the point of infinite thinness, the crack and the ivory wall and the Self holding on disappeared into the land of Unity. There was no sudden flash of light....just a quiet disappearance. As I look back on it, I don't think I could pinpoint the exact point of disappearance; one moment the Self was there, and the next there was just Unity. "I" was aware of it, but not as subject-object. "I" was aware of being aware of non-dual Awareness."

"So now comes the tough questions that you are asking: What exactly is the land of Unity? You say: 'It neither exists nor does it not exist; it is neither this nor that.' I wish I had an easy answer from my experiences, but sadly I do not. I can tell you that experiencing the land of Unity is profound, and that you know the experience is true once you experience it. It is experienced in an non-dualistic way. Pure experience, without there being an experiencer. But any attempt to chart the geography of the land of Unity with words will fail, because charting and words are inherently an exercise in subject-object duality. You cannot chart the land of Unity using the tools of Duality.

So what good is all this if at the end of the day nothing exists independently and everything really is a non-delineated land of Unity that cannot be articulated? Because once the Wall drops and you pass through the door of illusion into the land of Unity, you no longer can live in the land of Duality *in the same way.* That is, experiencing the land of Unity (through psychedelics or meditation, etc.) does not fully remove you from day-to-day living in the land of Duality. We still experience day-to-day life in a dualistic way because the wall of Self has not fully disappeared. But what has changed is that we know that this experience of Duality is, at the end of the day, an illusion.

How does this knowledge of 'Duality as illusion' change how we live our lives? Because we can now experience other human beings, and the mountains, and the trees, and the tigers as fully interconnected. What happens to another human being happens to me, in a very direct sense. If my actions harm another, I am harming myself. In the land of Duality, at the level of individual survival, tigers are tigers. In the land of Unity, you and the tiger are one. When the time comes for an individual to die, the individual can approach his/her death with greater equanimity, knowing that the arising and falling of an individual is like the arising and falling of a wave on the ocean. This is important in the Dualistic sense of individual survival, but not important if everything is interconnected in Unity. The wave will disappear, and the ocean will remain. I do not know whether the energy of the wave survives or disappears. I certainly think it survives, if for no other reason than the law of conservation of energy But 'what survives' is currently beyond my level of understanding.

Before I die, I hope to better understand this land of Unity. I am a very early novice, to say the least. But I have passed through the door of illusion and hope to better understand this new terrain before my life ends."

❈❈❈❈❈❈❈

(To the parents of my readers: this is **_not_** a recommendation to the addressees of this letter that they go experiment with entheogens. Though . . . .)

As you can see from the story and description above, there are a couple of additional commonalities which seem to attend such mystical states of consciousness. **The first** is the admitted failure of language to adequately and accurately express what the subject is experiencing. All attempts to put it in words fall short. They can point the listener in a direction, (cf., the oft-used "pointing at the moon" metaphor when trying to explain how statements about God can be meaningful) but they can't capture what has been experienced. (Which, come to think of it, is probably true, at least to some degree, of any experience we have.)

"It is not given to us to grasp the truth, which is identical with the divine, directly. We perceive it only in reflection, in example and symbol, in singular and related appearances. It meets us as a kind of life which is incomprehensible to us, and yet we cannot free ourselves from the desire to comprehend it."

– Johann Wolfgang von Goethe

And **the second** is the absolute conviction on the part of the person who has had the experience that what they experienced, revealed what really is the case. They have absolutely no doubt that they experienced something and that what they experienced was truly revelatory.

In any event, it can be pretty woo-woo stuff. Hard to get your mind around, hard to determine what sense it makes, and hard to see what relevance it has, if any, to one's life here and now. But what is clear about it is that it results in a conviction that "something else is going on". That the universe, your and my world, is not simply as it appears. All who have had such experiences, whether by means of entheogens or by way of various meditative disciplines, claim that there is an unseen world or reality which is intimately related to the world that is obvious to us all and which, in fact, gives that world and our lives a whole new meaning and importance.

Well, . . . if true that would be pretty important and, presumably, something you would want to know. But is it true? And how would you tell? There is some support for its truth in the fact that such experiences have been attested to at least since the 8th century B.C.E., they are alleged to have occurred in many different cultures, among all the major (and most of the minor) religions and over centuries of human experience. Somehow, that uniformity and recurrence needs to be accounted for. But happily, we (you and I) don't need to settle that issue right now. The main point of talking about this (mystical states of consciousness) here was simply to open you to the possibility that what they claim to reveal might indeed be the case. To open you to that possibility and, hopefully, to intrigue you enough so that you will want to look into it further.

The main take-away from all these different sorts of experiences, the main thing they presumably show (at a minimum), is that the natural world (the physical, material world that is accessible to our senses and their technological extensions) is not all there is, is not all-encompassing. Not all that exists, not all that we can experience, exists within its realm nor is subject to its laws.

INDIVIDUAL QUESTIONS

Now we come to a really interesting and different approach. I've been looking forward to this and I hope I have what it takes to bring it alive for you. What follows will be a series of questions (5 big ones) in which I'll try to expand your thinking, get you to ask: 'hmmmm, if that's true, then mustn't this other thing also be true?' Give it a try.

And the point of this is for you to see if your belief that X is so (where X stands for some statement about the way the world is) *requires* you to believe some further claim that you maybe had not even realized before. And specifically, some further claim that involves a *religious spiritual realm*. Think of it like trying to solve a puzzle, e.g. a big jigsaw puzzle. What are those other pieces that need to be there for the puzzle to be complete? What would they *have* to look like?

(When I say it *"requires you"* I mean it's something you'd have to believe or hold *if* you want your set of beliefs about the world and life to be both consistent and coherent. And, I assume, you **would** want that.)

1st **Question:** You agree, I assume, that **the four C's really are more important than the four P's.** *Why* **is that so?** What else would have to be true for that to be so?

"The four C's"?? 'What the . . .? Grandpa, what <u>are</u> you talking about?' Oops, sorry about that. I got a little ahead of myself.

The four C's are a grandpa-ism, a phrasing I've coined to provide a shortcut for talking about an important set of values and their contrasting set of values. The four C's refer to: <u>c</u>haracter, <u>c</u>ompassion, <u>k</u>indness and <u>c</u>aring. (I know, I know, "k" is not a "c". But it sounds like a "c" and I didn't want to ruin the symmetry of the name. Geesch! Gimme a break.) The four P's, on the other hand, refer to: <u>p</u>ower, <u>p</u>restige, <u>p</u>opularity and <u>p</u>leasure. Two different sets of values either one of which a person might strive to realize or achieve, in their life.

And certainly when they are stated in this fashion, I imagine that most people would say:

'Ohhh, of course I think the four C's are the better set of values. Of course, those are the ones I want to achieve in <u>my</u> life.' But how does one actually live? If we are to believe the social science pundits and academicians, then the two P's of popularity and pleasure, pretty much govern the lives of most high schoolers and even beyond high school into college. Then, when we're out in the world making a living, having an impact, power and prestige often seem to dominate the value hierarchy.

So, ...do <u>you</u> really mean that? Do you <u>really</u> think that it's better to be kind, say, than to be rich? Rich can buy you (financial) security, prestige, power, influence, even pleasure, at least for awhile. What can kindness or compassion 'buy' you? Perhaps a sense of self-worth, yes, and a little dignity? And you really do consider those to be more important, more valuable, than (financial) security, prestige, power, influence, and pleasure? Really? R e a l l y?

OK, I'll take you at your word on that. So what you are saying is that the four C's <u>really are</u> more important than the four P's, and not just that you think they are, or that your preference is for the four C's over the four P's, but that you really do think the four C's <u>are</u> <u>more</u> <u>important</u> <u>than</u> the four P's. (Think about that difference: not just that you think or prefer the four C's over the four P's, but that the four C's really are, somehow and because of what they are, more important than the four P's.)

But what else would have to be true for that to be so? If the four C's really are, in some objective sense, more important than the four P's (despite how lots of people actually act), what would support such a claim? What else would have to be true for that claim to be true?

Let me give you a simple example of the sort of thing I'm talking about here. Imagine that you were to claim that it's harder for people to breathe at higher altitudes (remember Grandpa at 8400 ft. out in Montana?), and someone else asked you why that is so. You might say to them that it's because there is less oxygen in the air at higher altitudes so we have to work harder at those altitudes to get the amount of oxygen we need to function properly. So in this instance, it must actually be the case that there is less oxygen at higher altitudes for your original claim to be true.

Well then, what else has to be true for it to be the case that the four C's <u>really are more</u> <u>important than,</u> more valuable than, the four P's? The first thing that comes to mind is that they would be more important if living in accordance with them accomplished some really good end for the individual (and for society?) which was itself seen as <u>more important than</u> any other end we might accomplish in our lives. So asking this question leads us to wonder if there <u>is</u> any such end, some final way-of-being which is thought (by virtually everyone? by most?) to be better for us (and for society) than any other end we might seek. Then, if the four C's were necessary for achieving that end, that would then support the claim that the four C's are more important than the four P's or any other competing set of values.

Here, then, are some of the answers that other people have given over the years to try to answer this question. You could adopt one of theirs or some combination of them, or come up with your own. Whatever you think rings most true and makes the most sense.

(Note: I'm not saying which of these possible answers actually is true, only that they are examples of what people have said in order to justify/support their own claim about the four C's being more important than the four P's. Can you guess which one(s) I think is/are true?)

Happiness. Happiness is that final end which is more important than any other end we might seek **and** most people who try to live by the four C's **end up happier than** most people who live by the four P's.

> (Hint: those who say this, e.g. Aristotle and most Buddhists (among others), don't mean by "happiness" what you might, at first, think it means.)

Because the sort of person you become by following the four C's is in some objective sense, a better **person**. (What could <u>that</u> mean: "a better person"? And are there any consequences for becoming "a better person"? See the next "Because")

Because living by the four C's makes for a better **character** than does living by the four P's, <u>**and**</u> your **character determines what happens next for you** (i.e. after you die). (For more on this thought, see question #3 below.)

Because if everyone lived by the four C's, **the world would be a much nicer place** in which to live.

> (The most common answer among secularists; i.e. people who don't accept or believe in any kind of religious spiritual realm.)

Because **all religions say** that the four C's <u>are</u> <u>more important than</u> the four P's.

Because **I can control** living by the four C's whereas achieving the four P's depends on at least some factors which are beyond my control.

Because, if I at least appear to live by the four C's, **I'll be much better liked and am likely to have more success in the world.**

This is a tough question. Don't be discouraged if you can't answer it satisfactorily for yourself right away. And, of course, more than one of the above 'answers' might apply. Some combination of them might be the case. Just keep mulling it over. What else would have to be the case, do you think, for the four C's to actually be more important than the four P's? And do any of these answers require that there be a spiritual realm?

> "Lay not up for yourselves treasures upon earth, where moth and rust doth corrupt, and where thieves break through and steal; But lay up for yourselves treasures in heaven, where neither moth nor rust doth corrupt, and where thieves do not break through nor steal."
>
> – Matthew 6: 19-20 (KJV)

> Sir Thomas More: "Why Richard, it profits a man nothing to give his soul for the whole world. . . . . . but for Wales?"
>
> – Robert Bolt[14]

❋❋❋❋❋❋❋

2nd **Question:** <u>**Do intentions count?**</u>

Huh? What does that mean? Well, what it's asking is: does it matter what your intentions *actually are* whenever you act or is it the case that the only thing that matters (other than the act itself of course) is what other people *think* your intention(s) are?

In our legal system, e.g., we distinguish between murder and manslaughter by the different intentions supposedly behind each action. In the case of murder, the murderer *intended* to kill the victim, whereas in the case of manslaughter, there was no intention to kill the victim, but whatever the accused actually did, happened to result in the death of the victim. E.g. they may have driven a car recklessly and that resulted in the death of someone. So *legally*, intentions make a difference in how we judge the action in question.

But what about outside the legal system? Does it matter what your intentions are or only what people *think* your intentions are? And to whom does it matter? And how?

For example, suppose you were really mad at one of your classmates and you wanted to hurt them in some way, not necessarily physically, but to do something that would set them back. Maybe you decided to spread a false rumor about them which, if other people believed it, would harm their reputation and embarrass them. So you do that but you make it look like someone else started the rumor. The victim then comes to you for sympathy and support and you give them that, but you do so because you don't want them to know that you were the one who actually started the rumor. Your *intention* in this case is quite other than that of genuinely giving sympathy and support. Does that make any difference? Anyone who might be witnessing your actions, including the victim, think that you really are sympathetic and supportive of the victim. You're a little hero to such observers. Does the fact that your intentions are really quite other than to be of help to the victim make any difference? To whom? And how?

The only possible "whom" in this case would, it seems, be you, since no one else knows about your hidden intentions. Well . . . not quite. One could also say: God. God would know. Yes, yes, I suppose that is another possibility, but we haven't established that any God exists. (True. But could this— intentions actually counting whether known by others or not – be a reason for thinking that one does exist?)

And *how* would it affect you? You intended to do something nasty to someone and you got away with it. No one else will ever know. Has that harmed you in any way? How?

'Well', you might say, 'it's had an effect on my character. It has done at least a little shaping of my *character* in such a way that makes it less noble and admirable.' Where what we mean by *character* here is: the habits and inclinations of behavior and intention which one develops over a lifetime. (In a religious context this is often referred to as one's "soul".) Yeah, and so? So what if you've formed a character a little bit toward the bad side (or, at least, toward what people conventionally call the "bad" side)? What difference does that make? Doesn't it only make a difference if other people know or perceive you as having a bad character? If other people have no idea of or a mistaken idea of your character, then they (any of your real but hidden intentions) don't really make any difference do they?

❋❋❋❋❋❋❋

What are you thinking about that right now? Do you think: 'yes, it makes a difference' or are you thinking, 'yeah, . . . I don't think it really does make any difference.' Suppose you find yourself answering in the first way, that it does make a difference. This 2nd question asks *why*? What else would have to be true for it to be the case that your intentions actually do make a difference even if other people don't know what they are? If your intentions really do **count**, it seems they would have to make a difference somehow, somewhere.

43

Puzzle over this one for awhile. "Do our intentions count?" But this time, no "possible answers" to get you started.

There's a fairly famous passage in Plato's *The Republic*, Book II, 358d—361d, that raises just this issue. (In *The Republic*, the focus is not so much on one's intentions as it is on the nature of justice and what makes people strive to be just, but in dealing with that subject this notion of our intentions can also be seen.) The story tells of a shepherd named Gyges who finds a magic ring which renders its wearer invisible when it is turned around on the finger of the wearer. (Shades of Frodo in Tolkien's tales? Whaattt? You thought that was original with Tolkien? I can assure you that Tolkien had read his Plato. (And so should you?)). In any case, Gyges uses this new found power to do all sorts of nasty things from murder and rape to regicide and taking over a kingdom. And Glaucon, who is disputing with Socrates at this point in the dialogue, is proposing that we would all act this way if we could. Essentially, that we act "justly" only because we could be caught if we acted "unjustly" and we're afraid of the consequences of being caught.

The notion of our intentions and whether they 'count' comes in here because we're imagining something similar to Gyges's ring. We're imagining that we could hide our true intentions from any observer and thereby get away with all sorts of dastardly deeds. And we're then asking: if we could actually do that, would there be any comparable negative consequences for us? If there wouldn't be, then it seems that our intentions don't really count; by themselves they don't make any difference. They only make a difference if other people know of them and either approve or disapprove.

So what do you think? Do intentions count even if they are never known by other people? And if so, how? And why? And if they do make a difference, is that difference really significant? And most importantly perhaps, does your answer here *require* that there be some sort of *spiritual* realm? How so?

Reputation is what men and women think of us; character is what God and angels know of us.

– Thomas Paine

3ʳᵈ Question: <u>**Is character destiny?**</u>

Put another way: will the character you've developed and formed over the years of your life (see the previous question for a definition of character) determine what will happen to you after you die?

(Note: when this question says: "happen to you after you die," it is not referring simply to your body. It is not asking what happens to your body after you die. What happens to your body after you die is, as you well know, a function simply of chemistry and biology–your body decomposes. Rather, it's assuming there is something 'in' you which is not wholly dependent upon your body but yet which captures, expresses, or defines, a 'you' which is unique and which is continuous with the 'you' that you know and cherish here and now.)

The first thing you're bound to notice in this question is that it *assumes* that something *can* happen <u>*to you*</u> after you die; i.e. it assumes that there is a 'you', a 'self', which exists now and will continue to exist after the death of your body. And we can't just go around assuming something like that. That's really big and we shouldn't just assume an answer to it. So let's not. Let's admit that this question is more complex than it might have at first appeared. It's really got a number of other questions folded into it. E.g., and at least, these two: do we even have a self that is other than our body? And, if we do, is that self capable of existing without our body? (You might think of such a 'self' as: your consciousness, plus your mental and emotional abilities, plus your personality, plus your character. (As mentioned before, that self is, in religious contexts, most commonly referred to as a "soul" or maybe a "spirit".)

Welllll, the first of these questions: do we even have a 'self'?, seems pretty easy to answer, at least in a letter like this (vs., say, some hoary academic dissertation), and that answer would be: of course! There is a thinker, decider, judger, perceiver, lover etc. that we identify with the shorthand "I". Your 'self', e.g., is the one who is currently reading this letter, understanding what you are reading and trying to make a decision about what it's talking about. Indeed, if anyone were to ask you if you have a 'self', the easiest answer would be: "yes, it's the 'self' who is listening to you right now, and that you are assuming to be here listening to you right now!!"

But note that saying this does not commit us to also saying that this 'self' is some one, unchanging thing. Pretty clearly, it is not. Our 'selves' seem more like a stream, continually changing but also having an identity through time such that we can recognize, both in ourselves and in others, that we are (largely) the same self as we were yesterday, and identifiably the same self as we were 10 or 15 years ago (or even 40 or 50 years ago for your Grandpa). Our 'self' illustrates a continuity through change that seems to be a prominent feature of virtually everything that exists.

The last part of that earlier question: "is it other than our body?" also seems pretty easy to answer since our bodies can and do change everyday and sometimes in large and significant ways and yet we say that we, our self, is still there. And supposedly every cell and even every atom in our body changes every seven years or so, and yet we remain conscious of a continuous self. So, though in our current, embodied state, our selves are in part formed and certainly affected by our bodies, they don't seem to be identical with our bodies or any part thereof.

OK, but what about that second question above? That's the hard one, yes? The question that asked: is that self capable of existing without our body? And here, I'm going to do a little side step. Rather than launching off into a discussion on that particular question directly, I would rather just point out that both of these questions are wonderful examples of how if you say or think that X is the case, you are then often committing yourself to holding that some other claim, call it Y, is also the case. In this instance if we want to say that "character <u>is</u> destiny" we got quickly involved in talking about something called character and a self and whether it makes any sense to speak of a destiny for that self after the death of one's body.

But suppose you want to avoid all those prickly questions about a self and a self independent of our body etc., so you simply say: 'Nope, character <u>is not</u> destiny. At least it doesn't lead to any destiny beyond whatever effects it has on us during our lifetime.' Well, . . . then you're thrown back into the position of saying (or at least holding) that it's possible, if one is clever enough or lucky enough, to commit some terrible deed and get away with it scot free. (Cf. the Ring of Gyges) No one else ever knows that you were, e.g., the agent or what your real intentions were, so there may, apparently, be no cost to you from or in this world. You can go merrily along your way. And maybe <u>that</u> <u>is</u> the way the world is. (For a movie version of this dilemma, watch *Crimes and Misdemeanors*.)

(It's a *dilemma* because it seems that we instinctually or naturally *want* the world to be fair and just; we want it to be the case that evil actions will at least at some point reap appropriate consequences for the actor. This desire is reflected in many of our common sayings, e.g. "As you sow, so shall you reap" and "What goes around comes around." Not to mention its virtual universal presence in most religions, as heaven and hell or karma and re-birth / reincarnation, and Gehinnom.)

Or maybe the self can and does persist beyond the death of the body. And maybe there is some form of ultimate justice so that character really is destiny.

> ". . . there is a "'higher' responsibility, which grows out of
> a conscious or subconscious certainty that our death ends
> nothing, because everything is forever being recorded and
> evaluated somewhere else, somewhere 'above us' in . . .
> an integral aspect of the secret order of the cosmos, of
> nature, and of life, which believers call God and to whose
> judgment everything is liable."
>
> – Vaclav Havel[15]

All That You Have Is Your Soul

by Tracy Chapman

"Don't be tempted by the shiny apple
Don't you eat of a bitter fruit Hunger only for a
taste of justice Hunger only for a world of truth
'Cause all that you have is your soul."

(Note, my favorite sung version of this is
Emmy Lou Harris's. Give it a listen.)

Hmmmm. So how <u>does</u> the world roll then? Do bad or evil actions sometimes go forever unaccounted for, as it often seems? Or is character destiny? Is it the case that as you sow, so shall you reap? And if you opt for the latter, that <u>there</u> <u>is</u> some kind of ultimate justice for the individual, are you willing to accept what it seems to require, viz. that our selves can and will persist beyond the death of our bodies? And it "seems to require" this because so many who commit terrible deeds escape anything like proportionate consequences in this life.

So in this case, at least, some kind of *spiritual realm* <u>does</u> seem required.

And by the same token, of course, if you opt for the alternative, that there is nothing like any ultimate justice, then you are committed to the view that people who do evil things, even greatly evil things, may indeed get away with it relatively scot free. And if that's the case, why shouldn't you try it?

"The arc of the moral universe is long, but it bends toward justice."

– Martin Luther King[16]

4th Question: <u>**Are moral good and evil anything real?**</u>

Do actions which we designate as good or evil actually have some characteristic which makes them *objectively* good or evil? Good or evil no matter what anyone else says and no matter how this or that society regards them. Is there is something about them which merits their being judged as "ought to be done" or as "ought not to be done" or "may be done"?

The alternative view would be that actions <u>are not</u> *objectively* morally good or bad. Rather, such descriptions are just a way we have of labeling actions we don't want other people to engage in. They are simply a societal convention and nothing more.

Well, we certainly call some actions/behaviors good and some evil. And as such, we are saying that some actions are ones we should do and some are ones that we ought not do. And most commonly, this is thought to be a function, a characteristic, of the action itself and not simply a function of the time and the society in which one lives. Thus if we were told of a society in which people randomly picked out little five year old girls and tortured then for the enjoyment of the mob, we would say that doing so is morally wrong no matter what the members of that society thought about it. We think that morally right and morally wrong are characteristics of the actions/behaviors themselves and not just social conventions. We think that moral rightness or goodness and moral wrongness or evil are something real and independent of convention.

So let's take this "most common" way of thinking and talking about this as true. Note that I'm not saying it <u>is</u> true, but only that for us to debate the issues between this view and the view that moral good and evil are simply societal conventions would take us too far afield right now. Then, <u>if we take this view of things as true, what else would we have to take as true?</u> (Going back to our original approach in considering these "Questions".)

Well, one approach would be to draw a connection between what is good for us as human beings in a non-moral sense, with what is required of us in a moral sense. I.e., if X is something which is good for us, e.g.

learning and developing one's mind, then we ought to do X and by the same token *we ought* to help others do X. And if Y is bad for us, e.g. intentionally harming our own or others' physical or psychic health, then we *ought not do* Y.

OK, but that approach then requires that there actually be things which are good, let's say beneficial, helpful, for human beings and other things which are harmful or destructive of human well-being. Well, that does seem true to me, does it to you? If so, then that's not such a hard implication to accept.

Under this approach, then, it seems that if we are going to claim that moral good and evil are something real and not merely a social convention, then we would have to also hold that there are some things that really are good for people and some things that really are bad for people. "Good" in the non-moral sense of they actually help human beings achieve some kind of fulfillment or fullest possible way of being a person, a human being. And similarly, "bad" would mean that such actions would inhibit or block ourselves or others from realizing our full potential as a human being. Well, that and the earlier connection we claimed, viz. that *we ought to do* that which is good for us (and others) and we *ought not do* that which is bad for us or others.

Hmmmm. That all seems pretty reasonable to me, does it to you? But to be really thorough, I suppose, we would have to look at the alternative position, the claim that moral good and evil are <u>not</u> something real but are simply social conventions designed to keep us in line and to keep society relatively smooth-functioning and see if that position has implications that are <u>not</u> acceptable to you. I'll leave that little exercise up to you. (Not so "little", actually.)

"It seems, then, that we are forced to believe in a real Right and Wrong. People may be sometimes mistaken about them, just as people sometimes get their sums wrong; but they are not a matter of mere taste and opinion any more than the multiplication table."

– C. S. Lewis[17]

As you puzzled over this fourth question, you may have noticed something. You may have noticed that this question: "Are moral good and evil something real?" seems to be related to some of our earlier questions, viz. the question about whether intentions count and the question about whether character is destiny. And you would be right in thinking so.

Generally speaking, we think that when we talk of morally good or evil acts, we <u>are</u> taking into account the actor's intentions. At least we are doing so if we are trying to determine the guilt or the responsibility, of the actor. But outside of a legal context, why would we want to do that? Isn't that 'above our pay grade' and better left to God, if there is any such?

Well, we might want to do that because in navigating our way around this world and our life in this world, we do need to make some assessments, some judgments, about the character of other people. Simply stated, if we judge someone to be of questionable or bad character, we'd probably want to avoid many dealings with them. And by the same token, if we judge someone to be of good and admirable character, we'd probably want to deal more frequently with them. And there's the this-world connection. Intentions count in determining one's character, and one's character counts in determining whether and how and how frequently we might want to interact with someone.

And the last connection involved here is that, yes, we could not judge someone to be of bad character unless their intentions were evil, but it would also have to be the case that their action itself was actually bad or evil. If there is no such thing as an actually bad or evil act, then it wouldn't make any sense to condemn someone for acting in that way.

So these three questions (#'s 2-4) **do** form a nest. A very tightly and interwoven nest of issues. They comprise a particular world view. If you saw or even just sensed that, good for you. But do they, or any number among them, require that there be a religious spiritual realm? How so?

5th Question: <u>**What makes a life meaningful or valuable?**</u>

This question might be of special interest to you. Given your age and stage in life right now, I would think it crosses your mind at least occasionally, along with: what do I want to be? What do I want to do in and with the rest of my life? What does it mean to be personally fulfilled? And what does that (being personally fulfilled) mean *for me*? Who am I, really? Who / what do I want to be?

Does it (what makes a life meaningful or valuable) depend on how you spend your time or is it independent of that? Are people's lives meaningful and valuable simply because the person exists, because they are alive? Or are they valuable *only because* of what the person chooses to do with their time and energy? Or is it both?

There seem to be a couple of distinctions here that we need to get more clear about. What makes a life meaningful or valuable <u>to the person involved?</u> And, what makes a life meaningful or valuable <u>in some universal or objective sense</u> (assuming that even makes sense)? Secondly, why do we say that all people are due a certain amount of dignity and respect? Is that dignity and respect somehow related to their life having meaning and value? For now, let's just focus on the first issue: what makes a life meaningful and valuable.

Concerning the first distinction above, imagine a case where someone, let's call him Tom, really enjoys and even just 'lives for' collecting found string into a mammoth string ball. That's what gives meaning and value to his life, <u>for him.</u> But would we want to say that that is what gives meaning and value to his life, full stop? Would we consider such a life meaningful and valuable in itself, so to speak? What do you think? (And remember, this question in <u>not</u> asking whether or not the person involved, Tom in this case, is due dignity and respect. For now, let's assume that any person, no matter how they have acted or are acting, is due a basic degree of dignity and respect.)

"We hold these truths to be self-evident, that all men are created equal, that they are endowed by their Creator with certain unalienable rights . . ."

– The U.S. Declaration of Independence

"Whereas the peoples of the United Nations have in the Charter reaffirmed their faith in fundamental human rights, in the dignity and worth of the human person and in the equal rights of men and women . . ."

– from the Preamble to
The Universal Declaration of Human Rights,
The United Nations

What makes a life meaningful or valuable to <u>the person involved</u> seems pretty clear doesn't it? Isn't the answer: whatever it is that they really **want** to do or maybe enjoy doing? If collecting string into a string ball is something they enjoy and want to do, wouldn't that make their life meaningful and valuable *to them*? Or maybe they want to 'change the world' in a way which they think will make things better for everyone. And again, if they spend their time acting in the service of that, wouldn't that make their life meaningful and valuable *to them*? So, whether it's something tiny and insignificant or something great and grandiose, if the person really wants to do X, then doing X is going to make their life meaningful and valuable *to them*. Yes?

It seems, however, that we could still ask: but is such a life *really* meaningful and valuable? If Tom wants to spend his life collecting string into a string ball or sitting in a field and watching the clouds go by, would we really want to say that his life is meaningful full stop? Maybe we would. But I have to think, we wouldn't. It seems to me that something is missing. Some greater impact, some effect or impact which goes beyond Tom's own subjective feelings, his own happiness in that sense of the term. Or imagine someone named Cathy, and Cathy really, really enjoys digging holes in the ground and then filling them back up. Would you want to say that her life has meaning and value? **Not**, I would venture to guess, based solely on what she is doing, on how she is spending her time.

So that would seem to lead us to an approach which says that for our lives to have meaning and value full stop, meaning and value beyond simply what makes the person *feel* good, there must be something beyond what we're doing or not doing which provides the basis for our lives having meaning and value. It's not that our actions, our life projects, don't count at all, it's rather that those activities don't constitute the whole story. (Or you could take the alternative view and simply say that some lives really **don't** have any meaning and value over and above whatever makes the individual 'happy'.)

And here, I think, is where the whole issue of a person, any person, being due a certain amount of dignity and respect comes into play. We shelved it, or put it on hold when we were just getting into this question, but I don't think we can leave it there. **Why** are people, **why** is anyone, due a basic amount of dignity and respect? (Assumes, of course, that they are, and that you believe that claim is true.)

Again, it seems, it can't be solely because of what they have chosen to do with their lives, with their time and energy. If it were, it's hard to see any connection between what Cathy (example above) has chosen to do with her life, with her time and energy, and that being due dignity and respect. So again, we seem to be led to there being some other basis, some additional basis, for all humans being due a basic degree of dignity and respect. What could that be?

Well, suppose you were to say that the meaning and value of a life depends in part, at least, on there being some grand, all-encompassing goal or end-state in which each of us, *just by being*, plays an integral role? Then our lives would have some meaning and value independently of what we do, of how we spend our time. Though not completely so. How we spend our time, what we do in life, obviously has some role to play in this. It's just that under this scenario, it would not be the only factor. And by the same token, we could support or justify our belief that all people are due some basic amount of dignity and respect because they play a part in completing some whole which is considered good and do so purely on the basis of their being alive and being a person (or maybe just a sentient, a conscious, being?).

But then this latter approach would, it seems, require something like a *religious spiritual realm.* Why would that be? Because to say that a life has meaning and value *even if* what you are doing provides no apparent positive contribution to society, then the meaning and value of that life must, to at least some degree, be **in**dependent of what you are doing, independent of how you're living your life. And how could that be unless there is something else that is true about us, something that cannot be touched or seen or heard or be sensibly accessed in any way, and yet which establishes that we, that our lives, have some meaning and value?

Such a 'thing', something that is true about us (and therefore about the world) but is not accessible to our senses, would just involve a *religious or a transcendent spiritual realm.* Ok, you say, but what might such an *religious spiritual realm* be? What could it be such that it would support or ground the claim that each of us– each of our lives– has an inherent meaning and value which confers dignity and calls for respect from others?

We've already mentioned one such possibility (above) when we said that if there were some grand, all-encompassing goal or end-state in which each of us, just by being, played an integral role, then our lives would have at least some meaning and value independently of what we do. Indeed, that might even be the main source of their meaning and value. But is that the only possibility? I don't know, can <u>you</u> think of some other way(s) in which we might support the claim that our lives have meaning and value **in**dependently of what we do, of how we spend our time?

And you might note that this approach to finding a meaning and value to one's life is actually a fairly common response to this question albeit on a different level. I.e. to say that a life, any life, has meaning and value just to the extent that it plays a part in achieving some greater good, some good greater than the person's own perceived well being or happiness. Then, depending on what that "greater good" is, it's easy to see why anyone's life would be considered meaningful and valuable. Viz. because they, their life, constitutes an important (an essential?) component of a desired and good end. Indeed, such a cause may even be seen as greater in importance than one's own life. **Examples abound**. From the mother or father who sacrifice themselves for the well-being of their children or their family, to the soldier who sacrifices himself for his buddies or for his country's survival and independence, to the doctor who risks infection and illness to protect the health of her patients or her community. And the list goes on. It seems that such lives take on meaning and value because they are an essential part of some good which exceeds in scope and importance the happiness or well-being of the individual.

So, let's go with that for now, at least "for the sake of the argument". We can then ask: is there any such larger-than-life, over-arching and good, goal or end state which is there for everyone, not just the parent or the soldier or the doctor? And the presence of which would enable us to say that every person, every human being, plays a role, an important role, in achieving this end and the end is good? Thus, the meaning and value of a person's life would not depend on any particular cause they might espouse, but would already be there for each to discover and would be (generically) the same for all.

". . . it presupposes the heart's spiritual awakening as the true work of our lives."

– Mary Oliver talking about
Emerson's first book, *Nature*[18]

Why would that last point be important? Because it would follow that the meaning and value of a person's life does not depend on their actively and knowingly choosing some greater good to be a part of. Doing so would/ could add to the meaning and value of their life, but not be absolutely necessary. And it's important because it thereby includes everyone. And isn't that what we want to and actually do, at least verbally, claim is so? (See earlier quotes on p. 56.)

This is quite a challenge. It seems to be that if we are to believe that all humans are due a basic degree of dignity and respect, then their lives must have some meaning and value at least in part independently of how they choose to spend their time. And one way of that taking place is by there being some grand scheme of things, some end goal, which is both good and in which their being, their very existence, plays a part. And finally, it seemed for that to be the case, there would have to be some kind of *religious spiritual realm*, since such an end goal is obviously not anything temporal or spatial.

Well, that was one way of grounding the claim that all lives have meaning and value and are due a basic degree of dignity and respect. But maybe you can think of some other way of grounding those two?

POSTSCRIPT

Have you gotten this far? Remarkable. But wonderful, truly wonderful. There are just two things remaining that I'd like to talk about.

The first is: has all the preceding merely gotten us to: "well, ok, it *could be* the case"? I.e. it *could be* the case that there is a spiritual realm, a transcendent spiritual realm. As a good friend of mine who is a convinced atheist has frequently chided/spoofed me with: "well, and it *could be* the case that an invisible Puff the Magic Dragon is hiding out in my kitchen cupboard."

I think all of the foregoing has gotten us beyond merely a *"could be"*. Certainly it has gotten us beyond a purely logical *could be*. We wouldn't have needed any of what we have looked at to get to a purely logical *could be*. One can start with that. If a *religious spiritual reality* were *logically* impossible, if it <u>could not</u> be, it would contain a contradiction within its very definition. It would be like a square circle, something that cannot be by its very description or definition. And we would know that simply by understanding its definition/description much as we know that a square circle cannot exist.

But there's a different kind of *could be*, and for want of a better name for it, let's call it the *really possible*. That's the one we're interested in. That's the kind of *possible* being talked about when we ask whether or not there is intelligent life elsewhere in the universe. And now we can ask again: has all the preceding merely gotten us only to: 'it's *really possible* that an *religious spiritual realm* exists'?

What are your options? They seem to be: it's *really possible*, it's *likely* or *not likely*, or *it is proven*. I think we can safely discard the last. Certainly we can at least safely say that no "proof" ever offered has convinced everyone. That leaves one of the first two and we've shown, I think, that the first can be assumed. (If it's not logically <u>im</u>possible, it's really possible.) That leaves *likely or not likely*.

And here, my favorite grandchildren and great niece and nephew, the 'ball', so to speak, is firmly in your court. Do you (each of you individually) think the preponderance of the evidence (we've reviewed some of it above) makes it *likely* that a *religious spiritual realm* actually exists or do you think it's *unlikely?*

"Darn!," you might be thinking about now. "Do I have to choose?" No, of course not. You can leave it undecided for yourself. But is that just wimping out? Or is it actually a way of deciding without admitting it, even (especially?) to yourself, that you've actually made a choice?

In any case, the question above (about the preponderance of the evidence) leads us to **the second** thing I wanted to talk about in this Postscript. And this second thing might help you make your mind up about the first. And **that second** is: "how, if at all, does any of this affect my life?" Isn't that where the "rubber hits the road" so to speak?

Does it (the existence or not of a *religious spiritual*) affect your life willy-nilly? I.e. whether or not you think it's true, whether or not you think it's likely or unlikely? Or does it affect your life only if you think it's true, or think it's more likely than not?

> If you want to pursue this last question beyond what I say here (and it's a truly intriguing issue), you might want to look at William James's *The Will To Believe*, a wonderful and seminal book by the founding father of American psychology and one of the "bright lights" from the early 20th century.

IF it is true, then it affects your life willy-nilly. But not necessarily on any conscious level and not necessarily in any way others (or even yourself) might discern. If something, anything, is the case then it has some effect on something else (there is no difference that doesn't make a difference), and in a completely interconnected world/universe, that means it would have at least some effect on you. (Think of "the Butterfly Effect" but not applied just to weather patterns.)

And much, much more so if the 'thing' being talked about is a *religious spiritual reality* since that is considered to be the very ground of our being. That without which we are not, and only within which we come to be.

And even if <u>you only think it's true</u> (think it's more likely than not), then presumably you'll act in some way(s) differently than if you think it's not true, and it will affect your life accordingly. And by the same reasoning, if <u>you think it's **not** true</u> (or unlikely to be true), then presumably you'll act in some way(s) differently than you would if you thought it was true. So either way, **it's going to affect your life**.

'Ahhhh,' you may ask 'but what are those "different ways of acting" that would be triggered (or not) by believing or thinking one way or the other?' Seriously? **Seriously??** Don't you think this letter has gotten long enough already??! Ohhh ok, ok, . . . humbly acceding to your constant and insistent badgering, I will offer you at least a short answer.

What results from such an awakening to the spiritual is an entirely new perspective. (To get a sense of how this might work, read a bit about the often discussed "paradigm shift" in science.) A perspective which says or reveals that <u>this</u> (world, or life) <u>is not all there is.</u> Something else <u>is</u> going on. That this physical, material world is not all there is. That our physical bodies are not all there is to us. But rather that there is a part of us, call it a self, or a soul, which is not material and which will persist beyond the death of our body. And usually also, that there is some ultimate reality with which we are, in some mysterious way, essentially related.

Such a new perspective leads to viewing your life here and now as, primarily and most importantly, an exercise in soul-making. (Recall the earlier Mary Oliver quote.) And <u>that</u> <u>does</u> make alllll the difference. (Refer back, e.g., to the four C's vs. the four P's.)

The take away: <u>it does make a difference</u> whether or not you think or believe in a transcendent, a religious spiritual, and from that perspective, the difference it makes is not only other than, but also greater than the difference made by the secular humanist world view.

"We are not human beings having a spiritual experience.
We are spiritual beings having a human experience."

– Pierre Theilhard de Chardin
(as commonly attributed)

'Wait a minute, wait . . . a . . . minute, Grandpa. You're not going to "get away with it" that easily. So just where do you stand on all this?'

Where do I stand?. . . . . . Well, I certainly believe that there is some kind of "ultimate reality", something from which all else comes and on which all else depends (for its existence). I also happen to believe that this something is conscious, intelligent, intentional and caring. Such a being is usually called God (or some variant on that name).

And the short answer as to why I believe these things depends on something called abductive reasoning; i.e. reasoning from what I have observed, experienced and thought about to what seems to me to be the best, the most plausible, explanation for it all. (Recall my response to Cardinal Newman's argument wayyyy back toward the beginning of this letter.)

But at the same time, I'm plagued by a persistent concern, viz. but is it true? Or is it all just something conjured by my imagination to make me feel better? As my English friend has said, is it just my version of some Puff the Magic Dragon hiding in the kitchen cupboard? And how would anyone ever tell?

So let me end this letter with **another story.** Back in 2015, I attended an international conference on consciousness that was held in Madison, WI.. There were many well respected and interesting speakers at this conference. One of them was a Brother David Steindl-Rast originally from Vienna, Austria. (David Steindl-Rast OSB is a Catholic Benedictine monk, notable for his active participation in interfaith dialogue and his work on the interaction between spirituality and science.) On the last day of the conference, they opened it to questions from the audience for the panelists from that day's presentations. (There were four panelists, among them Brother David Steindl-Rast as well as a couple of scientists.) They had all been talking, that day, about mystical-like experiences (as we did earlier in this letter). And I was plagued then, as I am now, by this question: but is it true? So I decided to put it to the panelists, and I asked: 'when one has such an experience, it seems to me that the key question is: is that experience revelatory or is it illusory? And how would one ever know?'

Each of the panelists took a turn responding. There was a Zen priest, an Anthropologist and a Bio-chemist in addition to Brother David. All of the answers were thought-provoking but I thought Brother David's answer was the most enlightening. He said: "I think that calls for peer review." (As you may know, "peer review" refers to the way in which scientific papers, articles and experiments are usually vetted to make sure they pass muster. Are the claims made in the paper genuinely supported by the evidence and was that evidence collected in an objective, un-biased manner? And this vetting is done by other scientists who have the relevant background and knowledge to make judgements in the area being studied.)

So what Brother David was saying was that any such claims based on mystical experience should also be vetted by others *who had the relevant background, experience and knowledge to make judgments in this area.* And I have gone, by way of their writings, to some of those sources. What I have found is that there is a considerable amount of agreement among such 'experts' as to <u>what</u> they have experienced (though it is usually couched in terminology that they bring to the experience from their own traditions), and there is virtual unanimity among them that what they experienced was revelatory as opposed to illusory. They all came away from the experience absolutely convinced that what they 'saw' <u>is</u> the way 'things' *really* are.

> N.B. A fun little sub-anecdote. The Zen priest's answer to my question was: "That's a *very* good question, . . . I think you need to keep asking it." Ohhhhh, how very Zen of him!

'Well then, George, does <u>that</u> satisfy you??!' Not entirely, but it certainly opens my mind to the likelihood that they know something which I don't (yet) know.

My warmest regards, 'little' ones,
Your Grandpa, and Great Uncle,   George

Some books mentioned (or not) in the letter and which you might enjoy:

Books you (ages 15 and up) could read now and may enjoy, but they are adult books:

The Space Trilogy	by C. S. Lewis
The Screwtape Letters	by C. S. Lewis
Siddhartha	by Herman Hesse
Searching for Stars on an Island in Maine	by Alan Lightman
A Man For All Seasons,	by Robert Bolt (a Play)
The New Testament	by various authors

Books you'll probably get more out of in a few years, though, for Jake, now is fine.

Man's Search for Meaning	by Viktor Frankl
Apologia Pro Vita Sua	by John Henry Newman
The Republic.	by Plato (Especially, the allegory of the cave: 514a-517a)
Miracles	by C. S. Lewis
Mere Christianity	by C. S. Lewis

Harder to read. (In their order of difficulty, from least to most.)

Kindness, Clarity and Insight	by the Dalai Lama
How To Think About God	by Mortimer Adler.
Varieties of Religious Experience.	by William James
The Will to Believe	by William James
The Doors of Perception	by Aldous Huxley
"Do Drugs Have Religious Import"	by Huston Smith (an article)
Bk. I of The Nicomachean Ethics (On 'happiness' as man's final end)	by Aristotle
The Marriage of Sense and Soul	by Ken Wilber
The Phenomenon of Man	by Teilhard de Chardin
The Divine Milieu	by Teilhard de Chardin

1. Ken Wilber, *Sex, Ecology and Spirituality*, Introduction, pg. 3 (Shambala Publications Inc., 2000).

2. Richard W. Metz, "Don't Throw Crack Pottery at Haunted Houses," New York Times, 1 Aug. 1996.

3. James W. Heisig, *Imago Dei: A Study of C.G. Jung's Psychology of Religion*, p. 6 (London: Associated University Presses, 1979).

4. Steve Myers at https://steve.myers.co/jungs-regret-over-i-don't-need-to-believe-i-know/ gives a very good commentary and analysis of Jung's statement, above, and most importantly shows what Jung means by 'God' in these quotes.

5. From Darwin's *Autobiography*, First published in1887. But note that Darwin's bottom line position was agnostic. I quote this here only to highlight his acknowledging the power of this particular argument (2nd sentence of the quote).

6. Albert Einstein, column for The New York Times, Nov. 9, 1930. But note that Einstein did <u>not</u> believe in God as conceived and presented in most traditional religions.

7. Freeman Dyson, *Infinite in All Directions*, Ch. 6. Gifford Lectures Given at Aberdeen, Scotland April– November 1985. (Harper Collins Publishers, Inc., First Perennial Edition, 2004.)

8. Dalai Lama, *Kindness, Clarity and Insight,* p. 75 (Snow Lion Publications, Ithaca, N.Y., 1984.)

9. Andrei Linde's essay: <u>The universe, life, and consciousness</u> in Science and the Spiritual Quest, (Routledge, New York, N.Y., 2002). (Andrei Linde is a Russian-American theoretical physicist and the Harald Trap Friis Professor of Physics at Stanford University.)

10. Ibid.

11. C. S. Lewis, *Miracles, A Preliminary Study*, pp. 94-95. (Harper Collins Publishers, N.Y., N.Y., 1974).

12. J. B. S. Haldane, *Possible Worlds and Other Papers*, p. 286 (Harper & Brothers, 1928).

13. Alan Lightman, *Searching for Stars on an Island in Maine*, p. 83 (New York, Pantheon Books, 2018).

14. Robert Bolt, *A Man for All Seasons*, (First Vintage International Edition, 1990). (One of my favorite quotes from this play. Thomas More was alluding here to Matthew 16:26)

15. Edward E. Ericson, 'Living Responsibly: Vaclav Havel's View', *Religion and Liberty*: Vol 8, No. 5, 1998.

16. Used by M.L. King, but apparently first said by Theodore Parker, a Unitarian minister and prominent American Transcendentalist in his collection of *Ten Sermons of Religion*, in the third sermon of this collection titled: "Of Justice and the Conscience" (Trubner & Co., Ludgate Hill, 1879).

17. C. S. Lewis, *Mere Christianity*, p. 7 (First copyright in 1952, renewed in 1980. Harper Collins, 2001).

18. From Mary Oliver's Introduction to *The Essential Writings of Ralph Waldo Emerson*, p. xiii (Random House Publishing Group, Sep 30, 2009).

Printed in the United States
By Bookmasters